THE SPECTRAL WILDERNESS

WICK POETRY FIRST BOOK SERIES

DAVID HASSLER, EDITOR

The Local World by Mira Rosenthal — Maggie Anderson, Judge

Wet by Carolyn Creedon — Edward Hirsch, Judge

The Dead Eat Everything by Michael Mlekoday — Dorianne Laux, Judge

The Spectral Wilderness by Oliver Bendorf — Mark Doty, Judge

MAGGIE ANDERSON, EDITOR EMERITA

Already the World by Victoria Redel — Gerald Stern, Judge

Likely by Lisa Coffman — Alicia Suskin Ostriker, Judge

Intended Place by Rosemary Willey — Yusef Komunyakaa, Judge

The Apprentice of Fever by Richard Tayson — Marilyn Hacker, Judge

Beyond the Velvet Curtain by Karen Kovacik — Henry Taylor, Judge

The Gospel of Barbecue by Honorée Fanonne Jeffers — Lucille Clifton, Judge

Paper Cathedrals by Morri Creech — Li-Young Lee, Judge

Back Through Interruption by Kate Northrop — Lynn Emanuel, Judge

The Drowned Girl by Eve Alexandra — C. K. Williams, Judge

Rooms and Fields: Dramatic Monologues from the War in Bosnia
by Lee Peterson — Jean Valentine, Judge

Trying to Speak by Anele Rubin — Philip Levine, Judge

Intaglio by Ariana-Sophia M. Kartsonis — Eleanor Wilner, Judge

Constituents of Matter by Anna Leahy — Alberto Rios, Judge

Far from Algiers by Djelloul Marbrook — Toi Derricotte, Judge

The Infirmary by Edward Micus — Stephen Dunn, Judge

Visible Heavens by Joanna Solfrian — Naomi Shihab Nye, Judge

The Spectral Wilderness

Poems by

Oliver Bendorf

The Kent State University Press

Kent, Ohio

© 2015 by Oliver Bendorf
All rights reserved
Library of Congress Catalog Card Number 2014015059
ISBN 978-1-60635-211-3
Manufactured in the United States of America

The Wick Poetry Series is sponsored by the Wick Poetry Center at Kent State University.

Library of Congress Cataloging-in-Publication Data

Bendorf, Oliver, 1987–
  [Poems. Selections]
  The spectral wilderness : poems / by Oliver Bendorf.
      p. cm. — (Wick Poetry First Book Series)
  Includes bibliographical references and index.
  ISBN 978-1-60635-211-3 (pbk.) ∞
  I. Title.
  PS3602.E4656.A2 2014
  811'.6—dc23
                    2014015059

CONTENTS

Alan Shapiro's marvelous poem "Old Joke" begins with a hymn to Apollo, a deliberately flowery one, right on the edge of parody. But after a few lines of praise to the god of art, the poet has something startling to say about the strangely dual nature of poetry. Apollo's music—the freshest, most beautiful song, the radiant harmonies—are in contrast to

what you were singing of, our balked desires,

the miseries we suffer at your indifferent hands,
devastation and bereavement, old age and death?

Isn't it so? Gods are permanent and unchanging, but the poet seeks the exact words, a harmonious line or an appropriately dissonant one, in order to make lyric of the body's experience in time. What could be more apt here than that lumpy, hard-to-enunciate word "balked"? It's an ugly word that stops the music, its clotted consonants suggesting a spasm or contortion—and therefore, paradoxically, it's an exact, even beautiful choice.

But there are other kinds of bodily experiences, too, and one of poetry's central roles seems to be to bring us into proximity with the bodies and subjectivities of others. "We are of interest to one another, are we not?" writes Elizabeth Alexander, and poetry makes possible a level of intimacy, of seeing-into, which I am not sure is possible in any other art.

It's a joy then, a gateway, the chance to come nearer to a realm of experience little explored in American poetry, the lives of those who are engaged in the complex project of transforming their own gender. I say "lives", but of course this book is about a life, a single one, as the speaker becomes a man. Not that he (or I or perhaps anyone else) know clearly what this means; It's not as if hormones magically create a self inflected by a culture's complicated and often contradictory ideas of masculinity. They change the body, yes, but Bendorf is far too smart a writer, and too well read in our era's theoretical explorations of gender, to think that, when one is transformed, the handsome prince who emerges will then know clearly who he is.

And he's a writer possessed of the imperative to connect. Bendorf's poems never feel merely private, in part because they're sturdily built, crafted things, and the purpose of such care is to bring the poem into the realm of the reader's experience. Of course the particulars of any life are specific and individual, but there are also ways in which whatever befalls us is an expression of our common, human lot. Each of us, Bendorf understands, is a body on the brink of change, and which of us knows for certain the body we'll be tomorrow.

The poem that opens this book, "I Promised Her My Hands Wouldn't Get Any Larger," says much about this poet's work. The title's evident tenderness has an element of fear in it too; if you go retooling the givens of the body, just how much will change? The speaker's self-studying research project is mock-serious, but look where it leads:

> I wrap my fingers around her wrist. Nothing
> feels smaller yet. Not her, not the kettle nor the key.

Love, it seems, is the ground from which this transformation will proceed. It is not undertaken without trepidation; what if the hands the beloved have known do grow, what if they don't fit anymore? If they don't, the poem's unexpected ending promises, this speaker will find some other way to ignite.

Most who open this book will have considered the pain of the intermediate zone. In a culture in which nearly every perception of another we have seems colored by one question—what kind of body are you, man or woman?—we know or can imagine the pain of feeling so wrong, so outside. What we might not expect is joy, and humor, and the life of passion that moves in these poems, a book of becoming, of faith in the future. Who can write a book of love poems now? Perhaps the difference between Alan Shapiro's perspective in "Old Joke" and the one expressed in these poems lies in this: Shapiro is old enough to know the body as a field of losses, the site where the self and time intersect—but Oliver Bendorf writes from a paradoxical, new-world position: the adult voice of a man who has just appeared in the world. A man emergent, a man in love, alive in the fluid instability of any category.

ACKNOWLEDGMENTS

I would like to thank the editors of the journals and anthologies in which the following poems, sometimes in slightly different versions, have been published:

Barn Owl Review: "Caper in Which We Masquerade as Braver Than We Feel"

Best New Poets 2012: "I Promised Her My Hands Wouldn't Get Any Larger"

Blackbird: "Blue Boy"

Cutbank: "Provincetown" and "The Woodlot"

Crab Orchard Review: "Thanks for Everything, Leland Cooper"

Drunken Boat: "Outing, Iowa" and "Split It Open Just to Count the Pieces"

Echolocations: Poets Map Madison: "Thanks for Everything, Leland Cooper"

Evening Will Come: "Wagon Jack"

Indiana Review: "Patrón"

The Journal: "Prelude"

jubilat: "Take Care"

Likewise Folio: "Second Winter"

Mid-American Review: "Extremophilia"

Ninth Letter: "I Promised Her My Hands Wouldn't Get Any Larger"

Quarterly West: "Call Her Vincent"

Redivider: "The Doctor Told Me the Shots Would Make Me Spin Silk"

Toe Good Poetry: "Inventory"

Tupelo Quarterly: "Make Believe," "Love and the Bodega," "No Billboards in Vermont"

Troubling the Line: Trans and Genderqueer Poetry and Poetics (Nightboat Books): "Call Her Vincent," "I Promised Her My Hands Wouldn't Get Any Larger," "Outing, Iowa," "Prelude," "Split It Open Just to Count the Pieces"

Verse Daily: "Prelude"

My gratitude to my family (especially Mom, Dad, Ani, and Opa) for persistent love as both this book and its author came into being. Thank you also to Ron Wallace, Lynda Barry, Meg Day, Stacey Waite, Caroline Manring, Jesse Lee Kercheval, Coco O'Connor, Quan Barry, Ellen Bass, Amaud Jamaul Johnson, Ross Gay, Hannah Oberman-Breindel, Sarah

Crossland, Zac Fulton, and Mark Anthony Cayanan. I am so grateful to David Hassler, Mark Doty, and the Wick Poetry Center, for shepherding this spectral wilderness into the world. Thanks also to the University of Wisconsin-Madison, for the support of fellowship in every sense of the word, and to my fellow Lambda Literary fellows, in whose pocket of light this entire thing was hatched.

I.

I PROMISED HER MY HANDS WOULDN'T GET ANY LARGER

But she's decided we need to trace them in case I
turn out to be wrong. Every morning she wakes me
with a sheet of paper. In the beginning, she stowed
all the tracings in a folder, until one day I said *I'd like
to at least see where this is going,* and from that point on
we hung them on the wall chronologically. When I
study them, they look back at me like busted
headlights. I wear my lab coat around the house to
make sure they know who's observing whom. If we
can ensure records, if we can be diligent in our
testing. I wrap my fingers around her wrist. Nothing
feels smaller yet. Not her, not the kettle nor the key.
If my hands do grow, they should also be the kind
that can start a fire with just a deer in the road.

SPLIT IT OPEN JUST TO COUNT THE PIECES

> One might consider that identification is always an ambivalent process.
> —Judith Butler

Call me tumblefish, rip-roar, pocket of light,
haberdash and milkman, velveteen and silverbreath,
your bitch, your little brother, Ponderosa pine,
almanac and crabshack and dandelion weed. Call me
babyface, kidege—little bird or little plane—thorn of rose
and loaded gun, a pile of walnut shells. Egg whites
and sandpaper, crown of Gabriel, hand-rolled sea,
call me cobblestone and half-pint, your Spanish
red-brick empire. Call me panic and Orion, Pinocchio
and buttercream. Saltlick, shooting star, August peach
and hurricane. Call me giddyup and Tarzan, riot boy
and monk, flavor-trip and soldier and departure.
Call me Eiffel Tower, arrondissement, le garçon,
call me the cigarette tossed near the leak
of gasoline. Call me and tell me that Paris is on fire at last,
that the queens of Harlem can have their operations
and their washing machines. Call me seamless,
call me sir. Call me tomorrow's inevitable sunrise.

MAKE BELIEVE

Make believe generally has no rules except to stay in character.
—Wikipedia

The first time I took a razor to my face

I forgot what I was made of. Having
made believe all I could, I made believe

a little further, pulling the open blade

around the corner of my lips, watching
a few desolate strands fall to the sink

like soldiers in a porcelain trench,

or as with invisible ink drew myself
a mustache I could get behind.

Or I am made up of fanciful scraps

and small fingers, one for every time
I've ever been called *Sir*.

Tomorrow I'll get a prescription

is what I've resolved every day since
the last June solstice drained the light

from the sky and passerines remembered

they had wings. In the woods I walk
figure eights around ground shrubs

that cling to the cold grass below

and remind myself: no guarantees.
It's true, some days I want the beard

in writing, want to know that when

I needle myself every fourteen
days, all the hundred jagged things

that give me away will start to shift

and this traveling itch will disappear
for good. But it happens as a gradient

so I wait like small hands cupped. I wait

in character, hips pointing the way,
shoulders broad like a wingspan.

I wait at the outskirts of regulation

with my Stetson and Wranglers for
the oak tree and the sheep herd

and the waiter and the goat vet

and the teapot and the snowstorm
and my father and my father's father

and the children I pass in the field

to see me as this new soft man
and for me to begin to believe it.

QUEER FACTS ABOUT VEGETABLES

In 1893, the Supreme Court ruled unanimously that the tomato is a
vegetable.

I know I am a nightshade,
it says to its own limp vine.
I know how to burst

against teeth
with my juice and seed.
I'm as small

as a thumbnail, no,
I'm as big as the harvest
fucking sun.

I'm fresh blood
on a small curled fist.
I can be a boy, I know,

but never a man.
I can be Sunday gravy
or a pickled green.

This is still the tomato
talking to the vine,
as told to me.

OUTING, IOWA

If you've ever doubted that a body can transform completely, take the highway north from town, past the crowded diner with the neon sign for pork loin sandwiches, and go left at the arrow for the lake. Can I tell you? The land where I was born was born an ocean, and that ocean born of ice. Researchers and floodplains have undressed its chipped-up secret: plates shifted, glaciers melted into river, into rows of corn that flipbook past your car. Park anywhere and follow the trail back in time toward the effigy mounds, the sacred piles of earth we've managed to preserve, and all that's buried underneath. I still bleed, still weep: what we used to be matters. Here's a brachiopod, here's me twirling in a gauzy blue dress in the afternoon sun. Trace these fossils with your tongue and place them in my hands, which will never be any larger. Lay your ear against an iceberg while there's time and sing to me its trickle. Lift a geode from the ground and crack me open. I'll sparkle so hard you'll forget you thought this land was flat, as though you'd never find the valley, bedrock, ancient sea.

THE DOCTOR TOLD ME THE SHOTS WOULD MAKE ME SPIN SILK

Along with muscling out my shoulders and dropping my voice,
    they'd let me hang by my own fibers,
invade distant islands with my gossamer webs.
    If I didn't want to ask for directions, I could leave a trail
of silk by which to find my way back. Along with
    narrowed hips, caught flies. Along with increased sex drive,
anchors. The doctor said my silk would be
    as strong as high-grade steel in six months flat,
that *man* would not be right—I might
    covet my neighbor's grill, and I'd still
burn toast every time, but spiders would begin
    to read me as themselves and expect certain things.
Humans prone to arachnophobia
    would come at me with wads of newspapers,
even a vacuum, while I dangle in my own abode.
    Do you understand? The doctor asks. Do you still consent
to the shots? Yes, I say, comes with the territory.
    I already know what I will want to catch.

PRELUDE

What kind of
boy
if just two neckties,

what kind of ship,
default
and markless?

My body yearns
for animal
and I wake
on dampened sheets—
what kind of
bed
if tampered
pronouns,

what kind of
cockcrow dawn

is this new me

warbled
from your frets
and bow?

Mother,
I have chosen
the name
you once chose

and when I arrive
fashionably late,

when Odysseus
crawls
between my olive tree limbs,
his guile hanging lower
than his brawn,

what kind of
knot
with two small hands—

what kind of
boy?

THE MANLIEST MATTRESS

They should never sleep on feathers.
—Sylvester Graham, 1834, from a lecture on chastity in boys.

The first Saturday of summer, I walk into the mattress store and say, "I want your manliest mattress." They sell me a wooden box in mattress dimensions. The first two nights, my back feels incredible. When I wake up after the third night, I realize I can't sit up. From my lying down position I call the mattress store again and explain my predicament: the mattress they sold me is no mattress at all. But before they can respond, everyone I know falls through the sky below me, including the mattress salesman. I say, "I'm sorry, I take back what I said." But it's too late. The line is dead. I disassemble the wooden box and lay out the pieces in front of me like a miniature lumberyard. I start learning how to build something.

CALL HER VINCENT

for & after Edna St. Vincent Millay

Let's try one more time: call her Vincent
and she will press against your lips backstage,
write you letters that say, *when you tell me to come,*
I will come, by the next train, just as I am.
Her first lover will disclose to a biographer
that she'd been raised a son
by a mother who did not expect her, who gave birth
just moments after an uncle was revived
from the brink. His name? Vincent.
There's a photograph
in which she already knows how to take up space,
Vincent's hands small, wrapped around the branches
of a flowering tree like the tree is hers alone,
like it only bloomed within the picture's frame.
The photo is from 1914 and she is twenty-two,
already the age to touch herself and not feel sorry for it,
to let the salty-sweet of ache deliver her.
She never traveled without Milton or the Bard.
She lived in a farmhouse
in a field and that field was in a forest. She knew
that if you settle somewhere beautiful
you will live more spectacularly,
with firework and flare, with dewdrops
that rest on morning blades of grass
when you find you are sore from the way you fucked
and cannot sleep, with a breath that sounds
the same whether born of ecstasy or darkness,
a gasp, a rush to take in the world
and breathe ourselves out, O, like a mess, like a man,
with grace, even if our finale is a fatal tumble
down some stairs, the literati hushing our name
like a sexed-up prayer: Vincent.

THE NO SHAME THEATRE

Think about how you lock the door,
cross the street and wait for the bus.
Are you scuttling? I mean, could the word
"scuttling" approximately describe
how you move? It's time, friends, to talk
about the body. It's true that the word
"hubris" is quite lovely. How's that for
separating the word from the meaning?
I saw a farmer whistle while he knit
in the corner. A whistle is a turbulent
vortex in the mouth. It's not just you.
It's this expectation that you'll grow up
and become one of those scuttling
commuters with a very large filing cabinet
and nothing marvelous to say. The way
to not get lost is with the body. I mean
your. *Your* body. Look at it. It's like when
you say the same word a bunch of times.
Boy, boy, boy, boy, boy, boy,
see, it's lost all meaning. That's what we do.
Boy, you say you feel numb most of
the time. You say, because you wanted
to be young, you wore the open window.
You hear a dumb thing like *the boy unfolded
like a lotus flower* but in private you think
that sounds pretty nice. It's a good story:
the blossom unfolds overnight, one petal
at a time. In the morning, nothing but
sunlight on the new parts. Ra the Sun God
slept inside a lotus flower. It ate him like
an envelope. What a scuttling commuter!
But I'll bet his body was beautiful.
I'll bet he felt it when the wind blew.

BLUE BOY

O body come inside my God.
Spin his name, there is
a gentle joy to be had
on the ground. We want
the wind to shake through
the holy blue morning,
want to walk our flesh
down the street, impatient
and in love first and last.
Here is the boy not broken
but asleep. Here is his
skin, which has never
said anything but yes.

-

A boy washes windows. In black leather pants, he sings
"Money can't buy me love, can't buy me love…"

-

What makes them different?
He stays in bed these
days not out of sadness
but its opposite, which is
the same as the opposite
of gravity. It was no
accident that she was
there first. It meant she
knew his heart through
seasons and loved
it still. And he loved hers
still, after seasons,
names of things, etc.

\-

Christmas Eve, he stops at the grocery store where a crowd
gathers listening to the radio. The country is at two wars.

\-

It's a classic story shape.
The hero leaves home
to weather a storm
and at the end, he either
returns home and is accepted
or he makes a new home.
When he goes home to her,
he calls it that. He takes
her in the kitchen despite
the company. The stove
boils. Daffodils open.
He was gone a long time.
Which ending is this?

\-

She starts to cry and says, don't turn into a man. If you
must turn into something, turn into a wolf.

\-

War, of course, assumes
two sides and this is why
some cannot believe
in it. O right eye look kindly
on the left. Stay, stay soft.
Now the boy washing
windows goes home

to his darling. And then
he leaves, which is also
a kind of going home.
The corners of his sheets
are neatly tucked.
He sleeps for a long time.

PATRÓN

Patrón skips
chemistry
to teach his mother
how to dance.

They tumble
along balance bars
while her pearled
dreams drip
to the floor.

They dance
underwater
in a room
of salty tears.

All the better
to dip you with
he says.

Patrón
she says
how you give.

Some floors
are better made
for grief.

+

Mother he says
I'd prefer
to grow up
diagonal.

She sets a bowl
of tomato soup
in front of him
while he
polishes his shoes.

+

I am waiting
patiently
Patrón informed
a snowdrift.

December
and he's learned
to dip cookies
one by one
in a cauldron
of chocolate.

Between his
fingers he lets
sprinkles fall
in the shape
of how his
voice used to
sound when
he laughed.

+

Patrón's mother
wished she could
be proud,

bring his cookies
to her church
friends. Brag a little.

Patricia, she said.

It's Patrón, he said.

Right Patrón
you know
your aunt's been
asking about you
what am I supposed
to tell her?

Tell her
how I am now
says Patrón.

Dishes breaking
on the end of the line.

Mother?

+

Patrón's been having
film dreams
wants to be
the one
doing all the looking.
He looks
down Eighth
for the 92.

The sidewalk bends
toward darkness
like the shoulder
of a man.
Remember this exactly
he squints
like a shoulder
yes.

On the subject of
complex characters
his professor had
asked for examples.

The dark, he'd offered.

He's told
that if something
finds the head
it is because it has
begun in another
part of the body.

He practices saying
here is what I *do* know.

I know I am Patrón
he informs the bus stop.

So when I say
call me Patrón,
who do I imagine
to be on the receiving end
of such a request
he asks the bench.

His humidifier
in the shape of a penguin.

His penguin.

+

Fish learn
from the water
to be fish
and it's wind that teaches birds
to be themselves.

For Patrón that leaves
fire or maybe earth
hasn't decided yet.

Once again
his old ideas ice cubes
on the tongue
of a Miami brisket.

+

Some days he wakes
up old as squash.
His boyfriend
says baby stop being
so pretty, says I've
made it how
you like it,
says darling let's
catch a matinee.

Patrón doesn't
respond
too busy spelling
out words.

l-o-v-e

+

His boyfriend
felt the fever
first then headache
then one day
he couldn't
swallow down
a cough
during those
overtures
he loved so much,
always liked
beginnings best
makes sense
when you
think about it.

Patrón he said
Keep me warm
in the night
Keep me cold
Asked things
of him
he could not do.

But who else
would have read

him the *Book*
of the Dead
between naps
such a sucker
for ritual
right up to the end.

+

Patrón sews
a neon hem onto his lab coat
and takes
to the sea again
this time with an 8 millimeter
video camera
and an eye patch
and only the memory
of being five
in front of the fireplace
his cheeks
like apples hot.

There was
a time *before*
he was afraid.

+

On an island
Patrón meets a girl
who moves
in none of the usual ways.

The island
you must understand

was beautiful.
The shape
of the extra-large sky.
The way the buildings
stood in pastels
and the water
was a kind of green.

I am Patrón says he.
Hello Patrón says she.

Throaty growl,
smell of rye,
her jaws carved
from a switchblade.

They sip gin and tonics
at the bar
then slip out
and dance in the dark
along the lagoon
which is by now
a late-August milk bowl
of slime and want.

They swim
like fish toward
a hand holding
something
they can't quite
make out.

Patrón shouts
ALIVE! WE'RE ALIVE!

Well there's more
to him than that,
I'm getting there.

She takes him
home to sleep
on her trapeze,

pillow made of
old clown wigs.

+

Patrón folds balloons
into shapes of bodies
he's been with
who were, as we
say it, on the outs
of things.

These balloons
made the bodies
look good
that's how good
they were.
They made the bodies
seem like gods
at the beginning
of their best day.

The balloons made
the bodies look like
orchids.

+

Patrón would tell you
if he could
about his life
in the circus
where late nights
he would sell
and contort.
He would tell you
about the choices
a young sailor makes.

+

Someone says
Patrón I know my body
is not lost on you but—

+

These days
Patrón's chest is held
in place by two scars
shaped like
rafts rollicking
on a wild
sea. Every day
he applies aloe
with one finger
before he
checks the wind
and raises
the mast.

Yes and after
the buzz

of late-night TV
crackles out,
he gives himself
a hand.

+

Patrón returned
in a sorrowed way.

His old ideas
melted like tiny
ice cubes.

There was
a sea at his feet
and then
another sea
he mistook
for an arena.

The longer
he was gone,
the more
salty waves
smelled
like cheering
crowds.

Patrón returned
to a yellow
toothbrush.

He returned
to a new
way to taste.

Where have
you been?
everyone asked,
but already
his words
had slipped
from reach
so he just
smiled
and took
their casseroles
into the sea.

II.

Who cut me from
    growing into a buck?

Who left me
    only horns and hips?

    Still, I am a good animal.

    Strong,
but not too strong.

WAGON JACK

Some days I wake up Wagon Jack.
In the mirror, in the shower, I am man,
my jaws the texture of steel wool.
Nurse of my imaginary, make me
soft forever. In my childhood bedroom
I am six with scissors to my hair,
studying headshots of Elvis to get
the sideburns right. Wagon Jack,
become me faster, lower my voice
like the wrong end of a hose.
In the city, I sit cross-legged on a
bench rubbing balm across my chest.
When I call out, all my friends
are there. Our glitter tongues
tongue whatever they want.
Our tears taste better than a spring.
Kindness looks like itself. My own
hands wake me in the night and my ears
train on the silence. There are no
scars. There is no bench. I am back
at the farm, my girl sound asleep
right beside me.
Knife that cuts straight through me,
take my distress too. I am marching on:
fifty animals to feed, a hundred
kingdoms to plan, sun is shining.
Outside, the goats are banded.
To be boys forever. In the timothy
next to the creek, Wagon Jack grabs
his hands, which are also mine,
and together we feel for new veins.
I get what I wanted. Soft forever.
Diligent records. Love. Even a pine cone
on my head. My situation looks pretty
good. Three baby goats, and a girl

who says we will drink only good
tequila to stay current only in
our own events. I learn more every day
about what kind of boy to be.
How to make my words fall gently
like smoke rings or silk. Big eyes
even when I sleep. Wagon Jack
tells me a pine cone is a charm against
the bad. Let's find out. Isn't this
the best? I'm not tired yet.
This must be the best.

NO BILLBOARDS IN VERMONT

Hard work in its horse boots
clomped toward us
down the trail to the cabin. We were
growing a garden, had been growing.
Our loft bed suspended us with books
to read after chores
while the lantern, sometimes two,
burned oil. We queer

Americana, we who
doubted whether
testosterone makes a man
while we crouched thinning dill
in the pickle patch.

We were working, working it out,
working until every animal was fed.
No play party or disco ball here,
just skin, scraped and eaten,
our muscles gnarled horseradish.
We were a boy
and a girl when we slept.

Work, rinsed of citronella
and dressed for dinner, was always
ready with a hand
to rearrange us. It palmed
us, weed whacked us,
flaked us like hay.

We were each a girl and a boy
when we worked.
Left alone in the field, we would have perished.
Duty called to us
from every broken bread,

from the hills and their goldenrod,
from the green mountains beyond that.
Tired was good.

PRECIPICE

I don't farm for milk. I farm for the front row
seat to things living and dying. The dead bird

    like a small wet sock in a cement crack
    behind the barn, crawling with hungry worms.

The goats' voices changing from high whinny
to pubescent music box and then to western

    station just below the dial. I farm not for
    the countryside but for the tumbling sense inside me

that everything has to transform eventually. My
masculinity is animal at best: bellowing hoot

    of a barred owl. The wren dad's song. Castrated
    wethers who will stay boys forever. There are a million

and one ways for me to look, but I only want one.
I teeter at the edge.

LARYNX

after Yusef Komunyakaa

The husk in my voice from the field
belongs to corn still moving
inside my head. At night
it moves like a chemist. It moves like gallium
in a sweaty palm.
A blue of oxygen
creams around it
in moonlight.
I stand with my hands growing at my sides,
while it moves
like a choir singing gospel. It moves like bone on bone.
It moves like a syringe
drawn out of a hamstring.
It blows like the soft jaws
of a birthday boy,
insistent as thunder. Spray of a whale
in darkness.
It moves like a rack of test tubes.
It moves like aspen
just after a storm.
It creeps like frost
on a broken windshield.
It echoes like a bat
in an otherwise empty cave.

SUNFLOWER

After Chernobyl, a process called "phytoremediation" was used to clean up polluted water. Sunflowers were floated atop rafts on contaminated ponds, with their roots dangling into water to soak up radioactive material.

To blood bank your aftermath, you made me float on water.
Someone pressed the fuck button but it only meant trouble.

Percreta is Latin for: I floated three weeks on a pond. On a raft,
because you had to have me upright. I thought I was too

bright and mild to need to be prepared. Particles traveled through
water and then collided with me, rough, unshaven, like young

backpackers who knew not what they did, who wore last night's
beer and cursed in another tongue. Nowhere but my roots

to take that reckless element. Radiation is a jealousy, it multiplies
with good intention. How can we ever say what we've absorbed?

I shined forsaken, was exactly the right yellow, shimmered
charismatic, bloomed regardless: I was beautiful. The thing

that might surprise someone is how both fast and slow
a meltdown feels. The angry stem. The ravenous tender middle.

COOPERATIVE

When I call your name from across the bulk aisle

I like to whisper-scream as loud as I can. *#@$%!*

One pound of agave ginger cashews is a decision

to let go of resentment and thoughts of revenge.

Jasmine brown rice is the weapon you love me with.

In the deli, I bogart the sample cups. This is my way.

When I whisper your name it is like a scream within

the whisper spectrum. I make up my mind re: letting

go of resentment and revenge. I do not want to chip,

do not want to attend the ravioli demonstration;

want only to select my tender type, which is you.

Find me in the snack aisle and massage my jaw.

Everyone will have to reach around us to get their

dried snap pea crisps and revolutionary chocolate.

I like to count how many days in a row they serve

the vegan mac and cheese. I like to watch it shrivel

in the tin pan. The comment box is the exact

size and shape of my feelings tonight, right down

to the weird curly tail of, after all this, desire.

KINDNESS NOT FOR ANYTHING

Kindness brings softness and softness brings a three-legged clover, brings three fields of clover and I want to have them all. My want wants them all. My want is a giant balloon and it's spelled ah. My want goes ah. Ah is a soft thing, a very hard-to-get-to thing and it makes you go ah. Makes all the birds go ah. What is luck if not for love, a very bright beluga. What is love for. It's not for anything. We love it just the same.

LOVE AND THE BODEGA

Love went to the bodega and said, look,
Both of us are products of the cold night air.
We could get together at dew point. I'll call you
Any funny thing. The bodega said, love,
I am in contact with a freezing surface.
A freezing cold surface is in touch with me.
Love scattered the bodega's molecules
Thoroughly. In the street, pieces of bodega
Strewn quite randomly. Some pieces ended up
In the lapidary looking like stones. Some pieces
Blew through the wall of the old dog kennel.
And everyone who worked at the record store
Was pissed because who wants, at minimum wage,
To have to pick bodega chunks out of the bluegrass
Bin? Love does, that's who. The bodega took it easy
In pieces in the blue jean pocket of love. In a chorus
Of whispers, the bodega said, love, I'm going to send you
In a straight line to the sky. I'm going to reach you from all
Parts of it.

AT THE CHALKBOARD

What's your name? she asks.
He erases one area over and over.

His hair curls around his ears,
he's as soft as a bottle-raised lamb.

She asks again: what's your name?
He blushes and looks away.

Why won't you say your name?
she asks. He says nothing.

She is on her tiptoes
drawing stars in the northern sky.

He crouches on his knees
erasing more of nothing.

How can I call you anything
if you won't tell me your name?

He erases some more dust.
She draws some more stars.

THANKS FOR EVERYTHING, LELAND COOPER

Waunakee, Wisconsin

In the morning after an all-night argument
they drive north around the lake to the state park
with burial mounds to get some fresh air.

She says, *It's so Midwest,* with all these signs,
and he shrugs and says he guesses so, in a way
that broadcasts his bad mood even though

he looks around them at the signs: Pet Swim Area
No Biking Cross Country Skis This Way No
Smoking Beach Parking Slow Down Welcome

and has to admit there is no paucity
of interpretation. They hike in further and come
upon the panther mound. In the sunlight,

through leaves the color of dying rage, milkweed
down spreading itself across the muddy trail,
dirt stretches out beyond them hundreds

of feet in either direction, containing ash
maybe, maybe clay, definitely old bones
of ones who were there first. In this way

they forgive each other. On the way out
he reads one final sign: the panther mound
was excavated in 1929 by Leland Cooper

and his YMCA camp boys, who left no
records and no artifacts. Forgiven because
of the historical precedent for the destruction

of something built in a ritual way. Forgiven
because the way what feels like just a dumb
mound of dirt at the time will someday be

all you have left, and you'll want someday
to reconstruct it, and you'd better hope
you (or Leland Cooper) remembers how.

THE WOODLOT

I practiced on a dead possum
    my father and I found on a walk
through the woodlot. After dinner
    I snuck back down to the woods
where the skull hung at eye-level
    in the knot of a tree and I said
"Marry me." The possum's other bones
    lay to the side of the trail,
buried under the first fallen leaves.
    Other days, I thought
I might ask it with glow-in-the-dark
    stars on the bedroom ceiling,
or on the chalkboard if she got a
    teaching job. We were, as they
say, not getting any younger. In
    the little woodlot in Iowa
under the quiet gaze of bones,
    queer theory nagged at me
like yesterday's nettle in the finger.
    There were too many reasons
why I was not supposed to want
    to marry her, but we wouldn't
have to tell. We could just do it.

EXTREMOPHILIA

Q. If you could be an animal, what kind of animal would you be?
A. You already are an animal.
   —Microserfs, by Douglas Coupland

God bless the man who, in a homemade suit
of fur and horns, trailed after a herd of goats,   ·
climbing quadrupedal over a mountain. God bless
his palms and soles, pricked and calloused, bless
the solo hiker who witnessed him from afar, God bless
the goat man.
      I am only goat boy, goats teething
on my denim, piss dripping from their infant
undersides, God bless these cheeky weed-eaters.
I say to them, *go with me,*
         and they do: boy
with goats in cabin, boy with goats burning
current events for kindling, boy singing Broadway
tunes with goats in the barn—
          I feed them bottles.
Feeding is a kind of love; if I do it right, it won't be
clear who's filling whom.
        Here is goat girl injecting
selenium, girl with goat shit and rag, God bless the girl
who, aproned, dirty-cuticled, led the goats back from
the wobbly brink, God bless the brink.
           Marry me,
goat girl, with a ring made of your favorite survival.
Marry me wild, in a pasture, in the weeds,
on a bed of hay (God bless the hay),
         and make me
a better animal.

In my mind, I beg our blood to work. To keep us loving
long after we've breached. I lean into your shoulder, not light
    like a shearwater, but heavy and insistent as the horn of a goat.
The dunes that separate our maritime kingdom
    from fields of corn are an elaborate set. The puppets may be
tragic, may be lonesome, full of gravity, but we are deliberate
    and afraid of nothing. We kiss at the bar, tequila heavy
on our knees, like whales identifiable only by certain scars.
    He slaps the water with his fin because he can, the naturalist had said.
Back at the campground, sunburnt, in the dark, we find each
    other's heads below the blueberry shrubs (because we can)
and we do so in the shape of love, which is a peninsula.
    We are setting up the rain fly. We are stoned and can't get it right.
We are inside our minds thinking, *I was almost an island.*
    It never does rain. I never do get bored. Leaving the Cape
on Route 6, we chew taffy and listen to oldies. Here is
    the bridge. We do not hit traffic. We do not break down.

III.

The "new wilderness" is thus the spectral realm
created by the going out of animal life
and the coming in . . .
　　—Clayton Eshleman

THE SPECTRAL WILDERNESS

I said *Meet me in the spectral wilderness.*
You said *I'll meet you in the spectral wilderness*
and bring a canoe. I said *Meet me in the spectral wilderness*
and bring a canoe; I will bring a folio of blank paper. You said
Okay, I'll meet you in the spectral wilderness and bring a canoe; you will
bring paper; don't forget a pen. I said *Okay, don't forget the oars.*

In the spectral wilderness, we grew ears like mushrooms.
We could hear things that were supposed to make us sick.
We smelled like something we didn't understand but someday
would. It made us patient. In the spectral wilderness, I still
had to strap on my pleasure but it was bigger. I peed standing
up. There was a house we loved in the spectral wilderness.
It had a rickety elevator and cracks between things and a yard,

so it seemed we would at last not have to choose between
gardens and goats and the affection of our neighbors
because we had forgotten to bring any cups of sugar with us
into the spectral wilderness, or eggs. Mostly we wanted just what
we wanted every day: some greenery, a base camp of our own,
& always a better way to remember the poetry
that came in sleep.

CAPER IN WHICH WE MASQUERADE AS BRAVER THAN WE FEEL

Everything is about destruction these days. Actually, deconstruction.
We pull something apart and still no cereal toy. I'm looking
through you. I'm on the side of reading. Last spring, we read Gilgamesh
aloud to one another on the boardwalk over the marsh, while
sandhill cranes ate tiny life from water for hours on end.
Their beaks were like display tanks from a fish market.
I could speak at length about the pleasures of removing a button
from my chest. To create the opposite of pinning something
on someone. We were a cruel irony to be too ashamed to talk about
our shame. Later that spring, we drove south to Iowa, through
those golden collarbones called Main Street. A coyote lay dead
on the side of the road. Time and oxygen had pulled it apart.
We brought our fingers to our lips to convey that what we saw
was sacred, but what did we know? We didn't know what.

Driving west with watercolor,
    I was a little skating pond.
      I left my accidental silence
    at the rug outside the back door,
wrote my name in crayon
    all over my children's boots,
      got stuck on the tundra
    until the ache thawed out.
I shall clean the wall of fruit.
    I shall wash the dishes once more.
      Road sign says OVID 9 MILES
but you and I never arrive.
Even so, no farmer is so
    inarticulately happy as me. We
      make perfect sense to the parsnips.
Sometimes, home ain't my
strong suit. Everyone can dream in blue.
    And as we drive across every state line
    I leave my name on it. *South*
Dakota: Oliver. Montana: Oliver.
Here's the bright side, the glass
    of hiccups, the world of good luck.
      Will you be a thing of glass for my body?
The breakable thing I will not break?
I know even without your smile
    you never get rid of canning jars.
      I've been home, where love is
paper-thick with maple syrup.
Just boiled down sap, and me
    earning the sound of your glory,
      live-streaming the hidden part.
    It's August in the body that I know.
How to do with wood smoke
    and our newfangled type of ice.
      This is how you sleep, in skates;

the thought of amber, archers,
cinnamon and horses
coming back to me like an analog podcast.
Idaho: Oliver. Oregon: Oliver.
What have you got? I've got snowstorm
and a fast-talker. Got jittery
and open road. Got more than
sunlight for the detection of a sun.

SECOND WINTER

I don't usually ascribe color to feeling but today I am attuned to the way

the window blocks the wind but not the sunlight as we sit here

reading the Wisconsin journal with a Duraflame log in the hearth I think

sometimes we need love that dull needle to unknot our snags

and back among the sawdust there is one particulate burdened with

the memory of how a pine grove smelled I know what the dust

feels for the cone and needle I want to always be soft for you dear

soft all north winter long I am hoping for an easy kind of feeling

the city was hard like a silhouette of a man holding a guitar

anonymous but always making noise it was like a shark

and I was one of those fish that plunges under sand

at the slightest hint of danger I was one of those girly boys

it's true in the city I was both I was Samson and

Delilah I cut my locks while asleep on my own knee

which suggests this way of being me is the same as

being set apart for God to the side I am both good and

bad with instant gratification which is why I left the city

trucked up north to Lake Mendota I have a pair of ice skates

in the basement have a way of sabotaging my own loveliness

I have a girly-boy limnology look at all these sensitive rivers

I say while pointing to my veins look at all these vacuums of blood

under the skin look at this landscape on the back of our hands dear

while we sit here our fingernails growing out the summer dirt

INVENTORY

They said there would be spiders,
    & there are—cobwebs appear

in my home like apparitions,
    ghosts of a heaven they said

there would be. And I have found
    good people here & even

fewer ways to feel alone,
    here where the tundra

swans make their layover
    from the Arctic: I

hiked to them after the limnologists
    announced their arrival.

Afterward, a friend thought I
    said *tender* swans, not tundra,

& the truth is, I couldn't say
    either way—were they

tender? I have no carnivorous
    sense of humor, but I

have been prone to talking
    about the heart, I admit,

which they said would be broken
    on arrival, though it

is not broken now, not
    anymore. I like to see

the white glue in places. I
    have lately devoted

hours of my self to learning
    how quickly a crayon

will break between my fingers,
    & it doesn't take long,

but God, it feels good
    to treat my brain

to cerulean, scarlet,
    tangerine & red

for it has snowed
    five days in a row

and everything I see
    is white, white, white.

And I have decided
    with regard to the swans

that they were tender
    like a snowplow,

or warm breath
    on a frostbitten hand.

IN THE BARBER SHOP

after a painting by the same name, by Ilya Bolotowsky, 1934

I go to the barber and say, Barber,
make me a better man. Make me genius.
    Make me patient. I want my
        skin to always be soft

on the inside. I want a fade
    in the back. To always smell
        like rhubarb pie. I want to love
my life forever.
    Can you do that?

The barbershop hums
    like the beginning of a bee.
    My barber is silent while his face twists around.

        He begins to weep. His weep billows
across the floor like a bowl of dust.

I begin to think I have asked too much
    but I remind him, I am the paying customer!
        It's not my business
what he does with the hair I leave behind—
    make a wig, a bird's nest, a mattress, or floss his teeth—
so long as he makes me look good.

        I am not weeping, he tells me from behind
    his handlebar mustache. I am making
you a better man. Rhubarb pie, et cetera.

    His tears grow cobwebs. Spiders
        come to rest under his swollen eyes.
        He shows me the back of my head
    and it's true, I do look genius.

I take in my hands
his clipper blade and here I am again, seven,
    sculpting three-legged cats
        out of clay and sending them to the kiln.

I always began with a single lump
        and squeezed a whole body from it,
tail, whiskers, ears.

Patient, yes. Rhubarb pie,
    yes. Genius, American, et cetera.

        Wait, I tell my barber.
I take it all back. Can you make me
    into a three legged cat instead?

    But he is already sweeping up
    the shattered clay around me.
Some other man is next in line.

I THINK I CAN FINALLY HEAR JOHN MUIR

"There is a young man from whom we shall hear."
   —Ralph Waldo Emerson on John Muir, after meeting
      him in Yosemite, 1871.

John Muir has come down from the mountains, I say to everyone I see, and I mean it. I tell it to the barista who jots down a description of me. I tell the man reading e-books beside me on the bus. I can finally hear John Muir and he sounds like a guitar being tuned. Like a mallet rapping on a wooden desk. He habituates on a different frequency. You have to kind of jiggle the dial. Don't everyone come listening all at once. I can tell you what he says. He says he's ready for spring. There's more, too. I'll tell you the rest if you have a minute.

THIS WOLF IS GOING TO SWIM SOMEDAY

It is hard to make friends with each
one hundred legs of the centipede that jumps
out at us in late spring, damp towels
after showers under a chrome sunflower;
something about how fast they disappear.

The body's own words are a language
I knew early but have long since forgotten.
Each time I try to remember is like trying
to remember the way soup tasted in my
mother's kitchen the day the protesters came,

and my love is a dolphin and she too
has a language part-forgotten, and I am a wolf
canoeing while she swims circles around me.
The shape she swims is the size of a hole
inside her no one, not even I, can know,

but I spend my days planting flowers
along its periphery, saying *look, honey, look
what we can grow, look what we can keep safe
in the shadow of nothing.* Human as a
sunflower, I am sorry for impossible things

but the fact that we want the opposite
of loneliness so bad we can taste it, like the body
of a grape jelly iris, not flopped over from its own
weight but just before that, standing tall, saying,
smell me again, I don't want you to go.

THE INDEX OF EVERYTHING ROUND

Devil's Lake State Park, Baraboo, Wisconsin

bucket of sand

    crumbled
        exoskeleton of an ancient
    seahorse

    packed into smithereens
        waiting for a slick
    coat to go to work

drill of the ice fisher

    everything auger I keep
        it sharp I keep clean
    the winter perch

    no muck this time
        of year we have a beautiful
    market of fish on ice

    I barter I beg on ice
        we are lucky to keep
    from falling through

lakeside hiking loop

    come down from
        the desolate rock
    haunted Ringling

    brother elephants
        and I walk beside
    the railroad tracks

train bellows
    its horn I will
soldier on

this is my trunk
    I tell the conductor
this is my heart

trekking poles in the snow

what on earth
    kind of animal
weighs so round

and more mechanical
    than a fox
I think it is

my watercolor sponge
    taken up on the wind
or my off-trail tracks

where I admit I
    smoked
to smoother ways

& here is the bull's
    eye I sing
here is the dart

GHOST DOG

Could you describe the light?

> It's sunlight straining through the clouds. It reflects off the dirty
> snow and ice.

But what kind of light is it?

> It is like frosted glass, or water muddied from a paintbrush.

And the smell, could you describe the smell to me?

> Damp, the way a body smells when wet.

> And smoky, from the ice fishermen's fires in their huts.

Now I want you tell me what you see.

> I see a blurry brown shape in the middle of the ice.

Is it doing anything?

> No, it's crouched beside a fishing hole. One part of it swings back and
>
> forth, left and right, at precise intervals, like a bobblehead.

Could it be a dog?

> It looks like a dog, yes, the shape is similar.

Are there others there with you?

> There are many footprints along the railroad tracks.

But can you see anyone else?

A handful of ice fishers cluster in one corner of the lake.

Three women passed on snowshoes an hour ago, but no sign of
them since.

And does anyone seem to belong to the dog?

No, no one calls to it, is that what you mean?

No one looks for it or calls it back to their side.

Is the dog hungry would you say?

It's hard to say. I haven't seen it catch a fish.

Does the body still need things when a ghost happens?

What do you mean?

You said it was winter, what are the colors?

Almost everything is white.

But are there any exceptions to the white?

Some grey in dirty parts and clouds.

The brown shape we have decided is a dog.

And I do see one red pickup truck on the ice.

Can you describe its red color in terms of the dog?

It's like a puppy's tongue.

What about your body, does it need things?

    I never understood the idea that the mind could be free from bodily
        desire

    As though desire is a shackle and some other part of us its prisoner

    But yes I am hungry all the time.

Does the dog seem friendly?

    Friendly enough. I'm not near enough to tell its present mood.

    I could go out on the ice and determine.

Are you always so eager to please?

    I like to fill a need when I see it.

Do you think much about ghosts?

    Not so much anymore.

    When I was a child, I heard many things

    Footsteps coming down the hall

    The bathtub water rushing with no provocation

    And once, a voice speaking.

What did it say?

    Something about idle hands.

Was it a voice you recognized?

Not at the time, no.

I was always conjuring things.

In the schoolyard I led my classmates in séances.

Devoured novels about the supernatural.

Were you left alone as a child?

Sometimes yes.

Always I sat in a window seat on the second story until someone
returned.

And someone always returned?

So far yes.

What is the dog doing now?

Its movements are unchanged from before.

It bobs its head side to side, like a burden made easier by shifting
the weight.

And what are you doing now?

I am walking along the railroad tracks beside the lake.

Limping because I fell on the ice.

I keep hearing a train behind me, a horn, its gears on the tracks but when I look over my shoulder, nothing but a naked railroad

and my own footprints added to the path.

Fishermen are drilling a new hole in the ice with an auger.

I miss things sometimes that I cannot locate in the heart.

I have said too much.

So it seems you do think about ghosts.

I am always saying too much.

I woke up ravenous today.

So your body does need things after all.

Truly I woke up not ravenous but hungry, which is worse.

Hunger is a duller ache. It never leads me to what it is I should
consume.

Tell me again what it is you see.

Two men in camouflage drill a hole in the ice, looking right at me. I
miss now the

women on snowshoes, though at the time I resented their loud
interruption. I wish

I would see them again now. The white and grey of the bluffs, like
my pale winter

skin. The trees like tender stubble. The truck, still the color of a
puppy's tongue. A

blurry brown shape on the ice, swinging its head side to side.

And how is it that you see all of this?

I am looking around from side to side.

And what color is your coat?

Brown, it's brown.

TAKE CARE

Sometimes I mistake the sound of my voice
for a rubber tire on the shoulder of the road.
I mistake my shoulder for an angle formed
by two lines coming together in geometry.
I mistake geometry for the way mothers
are the holy holy holiest of holes in the heart
and I mistake holy for a dried-up plant
rolled into the pages of someone else's vision.
I am just as full of shit as everyone, incl. you.
And I mistake my fullness for abeyance,
mistake suspension for an early spring
rabbit hiding frozen in the road—I am
not the spring rabbit, I know, but it's easy
to mistake my ears for tambourines; I am
good at them without expending any effort.
Once I mistook the tart infatuation of a
kumquat for another seedless calamity.
I mistake seeds for nothing all the time.
I mistake time for space, space for freedom,
sparkles in the alley for a sign that our
universe is sentient after all, and loving,
and will take care of those of us who pray
however mistakenly, not on our knees
exactly, but with our hands clasped
that we may be mistaken for believers.
I mistake my hands for belief all the time.
I keep waking up expecting them to be
someone else's, but so far they're only
mine, and when I mistake distance for
absence I tend to go astray. Like when
I can't tell if someone is walking away
from me or toward me until it's too late
in either direction. I wonder whether coroners
mistake knees for elbows the way my love
loses track of left and right. There are times,

or should I say spaces, in which I mistake
fire for work gloves, which is almost always
a mistake and vice versa. I want a compass.
I need deliverance. Good god, take me,
mistake me back to the soft shoulder,
which I mistake so often for the road itself.

NOTES

In "Call Her Vincent," the lines in italics are from a letter Edna St. Vincent Millay wrote to British silent film actress Edith Wynne Matthison.

In "Queer Facts about Vegetables," the Supreme Court case that ruled on tomatoes was Nix vs. Hedden; the Tariff Act of 1883 imposed a tax on imported vegetables but not on fruits, and the court decided that for taxation purposes the tomato was a vegetable even though botanically it fit the definition of a fruit.

Sylvester Graham, a health reformer who lived from 1794–1851, published treatises on topics as various as spasmodic cholera, bread and bread-making, and a temperate lifestyle. His lecture on chastity, to which the epigraph for "The Manliest Mattress" is owed, is perhaps most notable for coining "Graham crackers"; he suggests, among other things, a bland cracker as a means of staving off sexual excitement.

One section of Patrón is written after the poem by Cornelius Eady, "I'm a Fool to Love You," from *Autobiography of a Jukebox*.

The epigraph for section III comes from "Placements I: The New Wilderness" by Clayton Eshleman.

"The Forgotten Dialect of the Heart" borrows its title from a poem by Jack Gilbert.

"Second Winter" begins on a line by Frank O'Hara.

A line in "Provincetown" is after the line "I am deliberate and afraid of nothing," by Audre Lorde.

Printed in the United States
by Baker & Taylor Publisher Services